PSYCHOLOGY AND THE ORIGIN OF CIVILIZATION

David Lloyd Shepard

ISBN: 978-1-7360025-1-3

Psychology and the Origin of Civilization
GOBEKLI TEPE: World's Oldest Religion

ABSTRACT

New evidence suggests that Animals, not Agriculture, are the basis of civilization,

The great mistake of archeology is in thinking that only "domesticated" animals could be useful. Zoologists and Psychologists who understand *imprinting* have shown that even "wild" herd animals can be imprinted to humans at a very early age.

Changing their genes to make them look "domesticated" would have required centuries and is likely to have occurred only after they were already being herded by humans. Herding is easy if you imprint them to people early. Agriculture, without draft animals to pull a plow, or drop their fertilizer in a corral, would have been extremely difficult.

Gobekli Tepe may have begun as a trading center that became the world's first shopping mall. Those who controlled the trade, may have eventually become the rulers. Trade centers may have morphed into city-states, religions, and empires.

David Lloyd Shepard

PART I

GOBEKLI TEPE: TEMPLES OR TRADING CENTER or BOTH?

Gobekli Tepe was built six thousand years before Stonehenge. Organic matter, found in the walls, was radio-carbon dated at 11,500 years ago. It quickly became the greatest mystery of modern archeology. When archeologist Klaus Schmidt did his great work unearthing Gobekli Tepe, he declared it to be a complex of stone temples built by Hunter-Gatherers. No evidence of agriculture or pottery has been found.

Did "Hunter-Gatherers" really take time-out from surviving to come to Gobekli to build a complex of temples? If this many people lived as Hunter-Gathers they would have exhausted their food base very quickly. It might make for a very bad episode of *Naked and Afraid*, with all of them starting to die off from starvation after 21 days.

Are they temples? Is there a better explanation for the circular stone ruins at Gobekli Tepe in Turkey from 11,500 years ago? Twenty of them have been identified, side by side. What function could they have served?

Some archeologists have said that this disproves the idea that civilization evolved gradually. Some say it disproves the basis of psychologist Abe Maslow's *Hierarchy of Needs* about the most basic of human needs, and instead, they say primitive religion created civilization before agriculture.

Scholars have estimated it would have taken many hundreds of people to construct the site, although it probably took many decades to finish. In all likelihood, it began as much smaller wooden structures. We now know that Stonehenge began as a wooden henge before it became what it is today. The wood would not last, and eventually, it was replaced by stone.

It is most likely that the people who built Gobekli had learned early on to corral and raise young animals for food. This would have been far easier than hunting.

Without animals to pull a plow, or iron to make a plow, just using a stick to plant seeds would have been incredibly difficult. Without this, supporting as large a population that would be needed to build these 20 stone structures would have been impossible.

Grain from einkorn or barley would have blown into the corral, settled in animal poo, a natural fertilizer, then they would have sprouted into grains far larger and more productive than any found in the wild. It seems likely that this would have slowly led to agriculture.

IMPRINTING: The Clue to the Origin of Animal Herds

The assumption archeologists make is that the people who built Gobekli were hunter-gatherers, based on the bones of apparently "wild" animals found in great numbers. Yet this ignores what zoologists and psychologists have known for a hundred years, and primitive pastoralists for thousands of years, that all you need to do to domesticate a "wild" animal is to *imprint* a young goat, or bull, or pig, or duck to humans at a very early age.

Nobel prize ethologist Konrad Lorenz noticed that as soon as goslings hatched from an egg they would begin following their mother around. What would happen, he wondered, if the first thing they saw, was not their real mother, but instead, Konrad Lorenz. As soon as they hatched they began following Konrad Lorenz everywhere he went. After two days, if their real mother were to show up, they would run away from her and continue to follow Lorenz.

Years later, Eckhard Hess and his associates conducted systematic studies of imprinting in ducks. His graduate students found that ducks would imprint to anything that moved. How about a moving beer bottle, they wondered? So, apparently after emptying some long-neck beer bottles, they tied a string around the neck, waited until the ducklings hatched, and pulled it around. The ducklings fell right in line, following the beer bottle everywhere their new mother went. The stimulus that determined what became their mother, was whatever moving object they followed. That became their mother. They knew nothing of their real mother, they did not even know what species they were.

It turns out that the primary stimulus for imprinting is *motion*. Furthermore, this species-specific social bond forms only during a certain critical period after birth. The tendency toward imprinting in ducks, for example, seems greatest at about twelve to sixteen hours after hatching and if it does not occur within thirty hours from hatching, it may not take place at all. In Australia, widely known for their sheep herding, they tell the story of a family that adopted an orphaned baby sheep. He lived with people for the first several months. They decided that they must put him back out into the pasture with the other sheep, thinking he would join the other sheep. But in the sheep pen, the little sheep avoided the other sheep and they avoided him. He would stay as close as possible to the house and bleat pitifully whenever a person came out of the house. He was not a sheep; he was a people.

Long before Lorenz, our ancestors used the imprinting mechanism to domesticate animals. Sheepherders would wait until an Ewe gave birth to her kids. Then they would take a puppy, not long after birth, and put it in with the Ewe's kids. This has to be done within the first four hours after the Ewe gives birth, or it will not take. The Ewe will learn the scents of all of her kids, and then reject any other mother's kid or puppy.

The sheepherders would then double imprint the puppy, both to sheep and humans. As the puppy grew up with the sheep, they would accept him as a sheep. Because the puppy grew up with sheep, it would never consider them prey as a normal dog might (anything that runs away from you they consider "prey"). As an adult dog, the dogs have a more forceful personality than sheep, so the dog would become the leader of the pack. The humans would now train the dog to come when he was called, and all the other sheep would follow his lead.

More than this, because the dog now considered himself a sheep-person, when a wolf, coyote, or another dog came around looking for a meal, the sheepdog would bark and chase them away.

When cats and dogs grow up together, they do not consider each other as enemies, but more like brother and sister. Other psychologists have raised mice and kittens together. One even raised a chick with a kitten. The kitten would play roughly with the chick, rolling him around with his paw, but never attempted to harm the chick.

Any animal can be imprinted to any other animal, if it occurs when both are young. If they have grown up in the wild, they would never be able to imprint to anything other than the species they grew up with. Dogs reared in the wild with their real mother, could not have easily been lured into a camp to become a human

companion. But if found in the wild when they were very young, and imprinted to humans at an early age, would have made an easy pet.

If any mammals are raised with any other mammal from the time they are babies, they will imprint to that species.

We routinely imprint kittens and puppies to humans. If this were to happen when their eyes begin to open, they will imprint only to humans and their own species, when they first meet them, will not be recognized at all. If they do not imprint to their own species by puberty, they will react with fear to their own species as a novel stimulus.

The great mistake anthropologists make is to assume that they would only have been useful to humans when their bones looked like smaller "domesticated" animals. That assumption makes it impossible for

many to see how easily they can be tamed and corralled if taken in by humans and imprinted when babies.

It is most unlikely that Aurochs or sheep would have ever been bred to look like "domesticated" animal, unless humans had been corralling them for centuries and, **even without understanding what they were doing**, eating the more rambunctious when they hit puberty and leaving the ones that were the most docile, to mate and become what we call "domesticated" today.

Left: a few of twenty structures at Gobekli Tepe 11,500 years ago, some 6,000 years before Stonehenge. The function of the narrow walls and the exit/entrance may be to keep goats or other animals in a single line, to prevent fighting and keep them calm. We use the same method today in our corrals. Narrow slots are used to keep cattle moving in one direction and keep them from fighting. This narrow entrance is found in circular structures throughout Europe, looking like nothing so much as a Pez dispenser for goats or cows, which would have made it easier to move individual animals to their ultimate destination.

If the only thing you know about bulls is from bull fighting, you have an incorrect view of the nature of animals. Bulls in the bullring are kept away from humans and tormented to make them angry before they even go into a bullring.

If you want to see an example of *imprinting* with a 2,000 lb. Highland bull, check out the following YouTube example:

https://www.youtube.com/watch?v=i8IQEfDZYjU

The above video shows a cowboy who raised this bull around humans from a baby. He is grooming the huge bull peacefully, sitting on its back, caressing the bull who clearly enjoys the attention and, like any puppy, is very attached to a human, following him around.

A Young Highland Bull, tame enough to pet. This can only happen if they are raised from infancy around humans. Feral animals, even dogs and cats, raised by their parents in the wild, away from humans, would avoid humans as frightening novel stimuli even today. They could not easily be lured into a human encampment. But if they are raised around humans from infancy, they easily become tame.

The people around Gobekli probably learned this early, but it may have taken generations before they learned how to successfully herd, corral, and breed these remarkable animals. They depended on them for food, clothing, and milk. Today, we are scarcely aware of how this could have happened.

The horns of their ancestors were routinely found in the houses at Çatalhöyük and elsewhere, 8,600 years ago, more likely used as prized decorations, as ranchers do today, or in memory of a favorite animal, not as an artifact of worship.

The males, the bulls, were probably eaten before they ever got too big.

It is likely that sheep, goats, pigs, and ducks were the first animals imprinted to humans. The carvings at Gobekli show a row of ducks, all in a line. And many "wild" boar. The smaller enclosures, about 4' X 6' with a stone slab on top, look like a cage, perhaps for fowl or goats.

THE EVOLUTION OF CIVILIZATION

I. FIRST CAME HERDING. It was so much easier to walk out to the wooden corral to fetch a meal, than to try to hunt it down. Hunting never went away, it just gradually gave in to the human tendency to take the easiest possible route to prepare a meal; much like microwavable TV dinners and eating out replaced home cooked meals.

II. IMPRINTING: The first herd animals to be used were based on wild animals that were found as babies in the wild, brought home and imprinted to humans. What archeologists call "domesticated" animals would have only changed their appearance after hundreds or even thousands of years of herding. As the wild animals grew older, the males were likely harvested at puberty. This created the unintended pressure of *artificial selection* due to the older and wilder ones being eaten, and the cuter and friendlier animals allowed to reproduce. Cultural evolution (artificial selection) in action, without any need to understand what they were doing. Most likely, goats, sheep, and ducks came first, with even gazelle and Auroch babies being raised until puberty.

III. THEN CAME SETTLEMENTS. Gobekli Tepe, at approx. 11,500 years ago, and many other places may have grown up as a central market to trade goods; flints, tools, animals, etc. Likely, these places were also used as community gathering places, temples for sacrifice, and even places to hide from the severe cold at the end of the Younger-Dryas cold period; the fact that they were below ground level, and had a roof, would have made them warmer. Recently a hearth has been identified at one location.

We see something similar in the almost identical Kiva's in America built by ancestral Pueblo Indians. Much like Gobekli, the round Kiva's, partly below ground, have "benches" surrounding the outside. This was an architectural necessity, to prevent the higher wall outside from falling down, not for sitting. Likely, Gobekli had the same problem with stabilizing the outer wall.

The fertilizer, from animal poo, caused the grains that fell into them to grow bigger. At first, only small plots of grain, einkorn and barley, were planted. Women may have been among the first to cultivate these small plots and notice the value of fertilizer.

IV. AGRICULTURE CAME ABOUT ONLY SLOWLY. With herds at every small village, the threat of famine from the difficulty of hunting, led to fewer deaths from famine and more babies surviving thanks to animal milk. The ease of herding led to increased population growth, to a point where it was no longer possible to sustain a large population even with herds of animals. The villages, such as Çatalhöyük about 8,000 years ago, had an estimated population of 6,500 to 8,000. So... agriculture gradually became more important, due to far more babies surviving to reproduce.

V. YOU CANNOT PLANT MUCH GRAIN WITHOUT A PLOW AND DRAFT ANIMAL TO PULL THE PLOW. Using a stick to punch a hole in the ground to plant a seed is not a good way to farm. It likely never worked at all except around the alluvial plains at Ur and the Nile valley. Until they devised a crude plow and a harness for a cow or draft animal, farming would have been very small scale. Plowing was hard enough that it made men useful. Women and children could have followed behind, busting up clods and sewing the precious seed.

Everyone would have been needed to harvest, winnow, and process the grains. For virtually the entire of our existence, the work of men, women, and children would have all been essential simply to allow us to survive. During the "agricultural revolution" the larger the family, the more hands to do the massive work of plowing, gathering, winnowing, and grinding the grain. Only for a brief period, in the industrial age, do you hear of the "stay at home mom".

VI. NOT UNTIL THE INVENTION OF POTTERY, some estimate at about 8,500 years ago, was it possible to store the grain to last through the winter. Before pottery, mice and rats would have decimated any remaining crop, leaving no surplus. The surplus led to increasingly large towns, and eventually, to what we loosely call civilization.

VII. WAR. This led to grand theft farm animals; when surrounding groups found it was easier to steal the produce of the farms than to hunt or farm themselves. War followed. Walls were built. Jericho became one of the first walled cities, estimated at about 12,000 years ago. If correct, this would have predated agriculture, except in small plots.

Above: An American Indian Kiva, dated from perhaps 800 years ago. Note the walls supported by a "bench" needed to support a taller wall abound the outside. A hearth or fireplace provided warmth along with a reflection wall behind the hearth. It seems likely that the larger enclosures, also partly underground for protection from the cold, were used by the people at

Gobekli to protect them from the extreme cold winters at the end of the ice age. Although, only one hearth has been noted at Gobekli.

The 20 enclosures at Gobekli above share a similarity with the Kiva's in the American Southwest. Gobekli enclosures had a high roof compared to the flat Kivas in the Southwest, which were covered with straight logs and a straw and mud top. Gobekli likely had a raised roof, better to prevent flooding into the partly burried chambers.

PART II

IMPRINTING: CHASING OCCAM'S RAZOR
The Simplest Explanation is the Best

The round stone enclosures are similar to the circular stone "kraals" in Africa that are used to hold sheep, goats, cows. Smaller circular stone structures were likely individual homes. Larger wooden circles may have been corrals designed to hold the wild stock to make them easier to harvest when they were not being led from grazing field to grazing field.

Evidence suggests that the larger structures at Gobekli may have begun as a trading post, a giant Mercado Pulga (flea market) like the "wet" markets in China where people bring their catch; ducks, civet cats, goats, frogs, bats, snakes, fattened puppies, for food, or spiders and scorpions for potions, or woven baskets, tools, flint, trinkets, etc. for trade. Petra, in Jordon, grew up as a center for widespread trade. Like Petra, Gobekli and Stonehenge seemed to have little else to offer to justify such a site, although Stonehenge seems to have clearly been used as a calendar to aid in planting crops.

Would they need 20 rock enclosures for worship? They could have needed them to hold all of the animals and products that people were bringing in to barter. Inside the circular area are smaller enclosures likely to be useful in holding groups of goats or sheep or ducks or maybe young Aurochs?

Some of the structures are completely filled with inner rooms but little room for people.

One circular stone site, at Jerf-el Ahmar, has eight enclosures inside, waist-high, with no doors. People would have access to only about 20% of the interior. A similar one at Gobekli has six such enclosures. Is there any purpose these waist-high cells would have had other than holding livestock, ducks, sheep, etc.? If they held grain, rats would have made short work of their labor. This was a pre-pottery site and without pottery it would have been impossible to seal the enclosures well enough to keep out mice and rats.

The 20 structures at Gobekli do not look like temples as there is so little room inside to allow many people, especially with the series of small rooms without doors.

Above, you see the circle outside the circle at Gobekli. There is a narrow passage between the two walls that would make pigs or sheep or cattle less likely to fight and keep them moving. We use the same method today to control our cattle and sheep to keep them moving in one direction (see below).

PART III

ANIMAL HUSBANDRY AS THE BASIS OF CIVILIZATION

HERDING ANIMALS WOULD HAVE BEEN ESSENTIAL BEFORE FARMING

If you think that farming is just throwing seeds on the ground and waiting for the rains, you have never been a farmer. The likely basis of farming would have depended first on the development of stationary herds of animals, likely sheep and goats came first, along with flocks of ducks as in the bas reliefs at Gobekli.

1. Goats are famous for their ability to clear land by eating everything to the ground.
2. Herds of goats, contained in circular corrals, originally made of wood, would have provided the basis of farming by willingly giving up vast amounts of poo. That is the basis of fertilizer that is essential for farming.
3. Wild grains deposited in animal poo may have been natures first educational lesson by showing how crops grow better in fertilizer.
4. First farmers may have moved animals back and forth between planting seasons, using their previous corral as a fertilized space.
5. To plant enough grain to last through the winter would have been incredibly difficult without first having animals to pull a plow.
6. To plow a field without an ox or donkey to pull their wooden or bone tipped plow would have been an ordeal unlikely to produce enough grain to survive a hard winter.
7. It is a great deal easier to harvest meat on the hoof in a corral than it is to hunt them in the wild. Likely they did both, yet they would have depended for survival on their own herds. Unlike farming, it would have been far easier to walk down to the corral in the middle of winter than to go into the forest for the uncertain hope of finding a meal.

Archeologists say they had no agriculture at Gobekli Tepe, although they seem to have had troughs for grinding grain. If it is true that they had no developed farming for grain, it suggests that the origin of civilization may have been from the care of animals. Animals would provide food, clothing, milk.

Animal husbandry most likely began when early people accidentally stumbled upon very young animals in their nest, without their mothers, thought they were cute, and brought them home. The cuter ones, those that did not get eaten, might have gone on to reproduce, giving people the idea that they could control the available number of wild game without hunting and gathering. Life became easier.

Any zoologist or psychologist will tell you that if you take in a very young duck, puppy, rabbit, piglet, goat, or sheep, they will quickly *"imprint"* to humans, instead of their own species. Konrad Lorenz won the Nobel Prize for the discovery of imprinting in wild graylag geese. The goslings followed him everywhere as if he were their real mother. These wild geese remained tame, even when they grew up. Konrad Lorenz found that after ducklings had imprinted to him for a week, if their real mother came by, they would run away from their real mother and continue to follow him.

Imprinting became the basis of civilization well before agriculture was ever discovered.

Carvings on the pillars at Gobekli represent three ducks, all in a row on the top of one pillar with four ducks in a row at the base of a second pillar. Rows of three, apparently geese, are on another. Cattle, foxes, and a single cat, a leopard of some variety, decorate other pillars. "Wild" cattle, or Aurochs, are common, their horns used as decorations inside houses in Çatalhöyük, just as farmers today, use bull horns as a decoration over the mantle or even doorway.

In Australia, a family took in a baby orphaned sheep, fed it by bottle, and then, thinking it would go back to its own species, put it back out into pasture when it got older. Instead of joining the other sheep, it avoided the flock. It stayed as close as possible to the house and would bleat pitifully whenever it saw people come out.

They are all cute when they are young. Note the wooden pen for the young goats. There may have been many wooden pens around Gobekli, but they would long ago have rotted away. We see only the rock pens that remain. If these goats had been raised in the wild, without being around humans, they would be afraid of people.

Above are African rock pens used today to hold sheep or goats.

Possibly shepherds were the world's oldest profession. The Gobekli Cowboys might have been second.

Taming wild animals is easy, if you catch them as babies. Changing their genes to make them look like "domesticated" animals would have taken hundreds of years of herding in corrals to select the cute ones into such a dramatic genetic change.

It is a mistake to assume that domestication of animals had to wait until the large aurochs had been artificially selected by humans into becoming the smaller modern "domesticated" cows before our ancestors made use of them. More likely, they had been herding wild animals for hundreds of years before any genetic changes were selected that would lead to what we call "domesticated".

All of these, the boars, gazelles, goats, ducks, aurochs, etc. might be misinterpreted by today's archeologists as "wild" animals when they found their bones; indicating that the sites around Gobekli were peopled by Hunter-Gatherers.

Instead, these remains may be evidence of people raising wild animals to feed the village. "Wild" does not mean they were hunted.

More people are killed by water buffalo in Southeast Asia, than any other species, yet when raised from birth, they become gentle farm animals, even pets.

Long before "domesticated" animals, the wild animals would have been captured as babies in the wild, and raised in captivity. This would have insured that they would be relatively tame by being imprinted to humans. Adult animals raised in the wild, could never be used for such a purpose.

Before they ever grew up, the older males would have been the first to be eaten, even before they got old enough to be dangerous or rambunctious. Even today, the male chicken are eaten first, it only takes one rooster to fertilize 30 hens. Over hundreds of years the sheep or goats or Aurochs would have gradually become what we call "domesticated", the smaller, tamer version, because they would have been the last to be eaten, hence, more likely to reproduce.

The tamest could have been trained from an early age to not only imprint to humans, but to carry burdens and eventually to pull plows.

This "modern" Scottish Highland breed would have taken hundreds of years to select for their genes to become a new breed, possibly from the original Aurochs. The Aurochs stood 5 ¾ feet tall at the shoulder, about ¾ foot taller than a Highland breed. Yet there is no reason to assume that domestication required making them smaller to qualify as "domesticated".

Young Highland breed in a wood corral, tame enough to hand feed.

At village sites outside of Gobekli, they have found circular stone areas, without the pillars, that could have been used for the town's corral for domesticated goats, etc. At Asikli Tepe they have reconstructed small, round wooden corrals that would have been used to hold animals. Older wooden structures would have long ago rotted away.

MULTIPLE TYPES OF CIRCULAR ENCLOSURES

- The smaller circles of stones often seem to indicate individual houses.

- Larger circles may have been used for containing livestock.

- The very large circular enclosures at Gobekli are quite similar to the Kivas of Native Americans in the southwest. Even the interior of these Kivas look similar, with "benches" surrounding the inside of the walls. These "benches", in both types, are structurally essential to keep the taller walls from collapsing.

- It seems likely that the Kivas and the structures at Gobeklli would have been used in the harsh winter to house many people to share their body heat in such an enclosure. Any one who has ever slept in an old canvas Army tent knows that just the shared body heat alone will keep you rather warm down to freezing.

- The addition of a fire in the stone enclosures would have made it possible to live through a tough winter.

- It seems likely that larger stone structures served double duty as a refuge in winter, a trading post in summer, a theater for story tellers or shaman, and a religious center periodically.

NEW PERSPECTIVE AT GOBEKLI

Klaus Schmidt had noted the presence of many cattle and gazelle bones at Gobekli, thinking it was indicative of great feasts. The feasts, he said, could be what lured people in to work on the temple. Similar "feasts" were found at Stonehenge.

In structure C at Gobekli, and at Navali Cori, there is a long, narrow entrance with a narrow spiral curve around the center. This evidence is missing from all of the early photos but has been reconstructed by National Geographic and the Turkey Information Center.

The next picture is the circular chutes developed by Dr. Temple Grandin for use with cattle that appear very similar to the double wall at Gobekli.

We use cattle chutes to this day to calm cattle as they are brought into a central area for processing. The narrow passage reduces the likelihood of fighting and escape and keeps them headed in one direction, like "blinders" on a horse. The close contact provides "contact comfort" that helps keep them calm. The high walls help keep the cattle from spooking.

It seems more likely that the double walled circles around Gobekli and the 40 similar double walled wooden structures found in Austria, were all used to make it easier to control the processing of their herds.

Above, the spiral chutes that Dr. Grandin developed for use with today's cattle. The narrow chutes keep the animals, cattle or sheep, from bolting, or fighting, by channeling them through to where they are going one at a time in single file. Dr. Grandin found that the narrow walls keep the animals calm.

See the next picture of such a mechanism.

At Gobekli, the narrow outer wall could have served the same purpose.

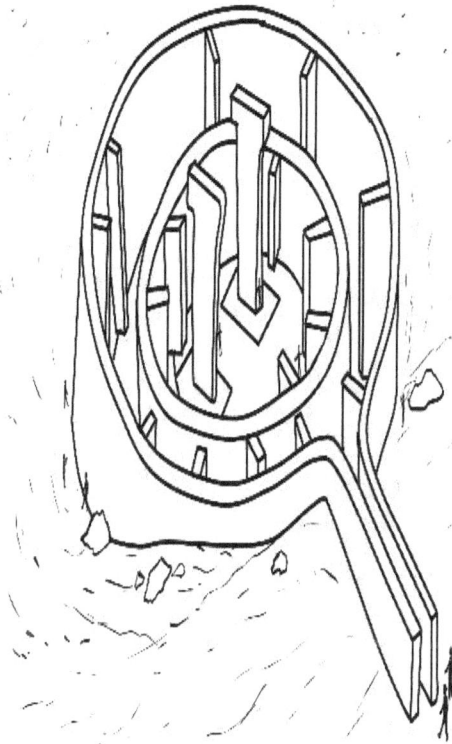

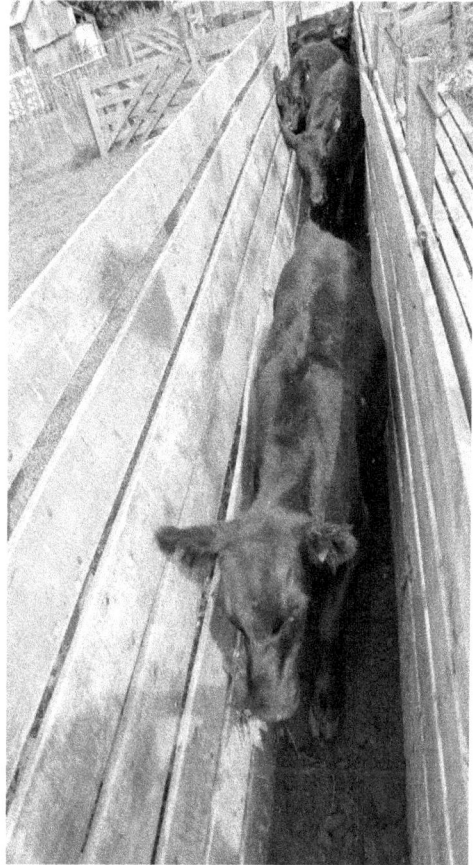

Wolfgang Neubauer reconstructed one of the 40 double walled enclosures found in Austria that seems closer to the purpose of a control mechanism for sheep, gazelles, or cattle. Other rock enclosures in England have a short "Pez" dispenser opening that would also have been useful for controlling the movement of livestock through a narrow opening one-by-one, into whatever they were using them for.

Compare that to the long narrow chute leading to the double walled outside circle at structure C. This long structure was not shown in the earlier pictures of Gobekli, and is still unknown to many. Even the second wall surrounding structure C was not in most photos of this site, and seems to have been ignored until recently.

Next is an artist's reconstruction of the complex at Gobekli, showing the relatively new narrow passage that leads to the double inner circle.

In the above picture you see a modern cattle chute. If you look closely you will see the inner circle (above right), as at Gobeki. Only the metal posts are visible in the photo, the barbed wire that forms the inner circle is too hard to see, yet it is a double ring, much like at Gobekli.

At the bottom of the above picture you see a view rarely seen in the photos of Gobekli. Other photos concentrate on the massive stone pillars in the center. At the bottom above you see three smaller stone enclosures just outside the main structure. On the bottom left, the bottom center and the bottom right are small, separate pens, with no entrance. These are too small for human habitation. What would they have been used for? Maybe ducks, young sheep, etc.? It seems most likely, they were pens to hold livestock.

Dig, dig, dig. The story is underground, in the towns around Gobekli and maybe Stonehenge. Similar discoveries around Stonehenge may suggest it also began as a trading center that morphed into a sky calendar and ceremonial center, although the evidence is far from clear. Whatever wooden corrals they may have used have left no trace.

One possible way to determine what was happening is to date the age of the most Aurochs and gazelle bones found at Gobekli. If the bones indicate the majority of the bones were of juvenile males, that might suggest that they were being sacrificed at puberty, while females and younger animals were still being herded. Again, just as we eat the Roosters first, because we need the hens for eggs, etc.

There are at least eight small towns around Gobekli. People may have traveled miles to Gobekli, because it began as a trading center that then became the world's first stone Walmart.

Similar centers sprang up like corner grocery stores across the continent. There they traded goods; flint, goats, tools, foxes, baskets (like the three on top of the 'vulture' pillar), ducks, grain, trinkets; anything they could catch, make, gather, or breed.

As it grew, Gobekli may have morphed into triple duty as a shopping center, a social gathering place (like churches today) and a sacrificial site as well; where people may have been expected to contribute perhaps 10% of all they had, to gain the favor of the gods, and help build the shopping mall.

If towns first began based on animal husbandry, these towns may have been the base around which we first learned we could plant wheat and barley and reap even greater rewards from farming. Grasses would have first been used as animal feed. Grains may have fallen into animal manure, and early farmers would have observed that they grew more readily with such fertilizer.

Gradually, grains became a major food for us as we ground the grains into flour for unleavened bread.

Animals would have been the first reason for building corrals and homes. *As in the settlement of the American West, cows and sheep came before farming.*

Herding is easy. All it takes is to catch young animals, imprint them to humans, and raise them in a corral. Hunting is very hard. Agriculture is extremely hard. It would not have taken long for our ancestors to see this.

Staying in one place would be essential for the development of agriculture. Having a herd to draw from would have been a great advance for civilization.

PART V

11,500 YEARS FROM NOW:
An Archeologist Discovers America

"...if the only tool you have is a hammer, everything looks like a nail."

Psychologist Abe Maslow

Archeologists are so accustomed to looking at temples, even a shopping center may look like a church.   With apologies to the previous work of others, including Horace Miner's 1956 article "Body Ritual Among the Nacirema."

Are these really temples? In another 11,500 years, after the next apocalypse, future archeologists would unearth our civilization and discover large oval structures at every one of our schools, colleges, and towns. Larger oval arenas could hold up to 115,000 worshipers. What could they be except centers of worship? Children are initiated into this rite beginning in the public schools, and continuing into the colleges, culminating in the vast oval chambers of worship found in every major city, and most schools in a smaller version.

On the broad green alter, two groups of eleven disciples compete to save the sacred Ancestral Skull, encased in protective Aurochs' skin. Eleven was a sacred number in America; clearly referring to the twelve disciples, minus Judas. Videos from the era show tens of thousands of religious worshipers spontaneously erupt in paroxysms of spiritual passion for no apparent reason.

Like the Australian Aborigines, the disciples would be seen as representing their tribal animal totems they may have eaten; the Detroit Lions, the L. A.

Rams, the Miami Dolphins. Occasionally there would be tribal groups that made no sense, like the Dallas Cowboys. No one could figure out what animal spirit they worshiped. Or what they ate. Dead Cowboys?

Videos from our time would show scantily clad vestal virgins erupting in screaming bouts of religious frenzy at unpredictable periods. These vestal virgins would chant spiritual incantations no one would be able to decipher;

"Rah, rah, ree-- kick 'em in the knee
Rah, rah, ras-- kick 'em in the other knee."

Bands would play and majorettes strut, in homage to the courage of the demigods who freely sacrificed their blood and brains as tribute to the gods on the great green alter of the temple.

Upright wooden pillars were placed at the ends of the stadium, signifying the passage of the Ancestral Head into the afterlife. As the fad spread, the wooden posts were replaced by upright steel pillars, with appropriate padding, to make it more likely to survive the enthusiastic disciples banging their heads against the sacred pillar in unbridled enthusiasm.

At the very top of the most majestic temples, an opening in the roof created a solar sky clock. Every day, at a sacred hour, the sun would shine through this opening spreading its rays upon the sacrificial field, which glowed a strange greenish blue. Spectral analysis of the field finds it is apparently not real, but an artificial substance possibly supplied by Ancient Aliens.

When the sun reached an undetermined spot on the lines of the field, signified by the Sacred Number 12, it would trigger a mass movement. This would signal every worshiper across the land to suddenly stop whatever they were doing for a sacrifice to the gods.

One of their major oracles was Sigmund Freud. Throughout the world, enormous numbers of buildings were erected in his honor and in competition to see who could be the biggest, the tallest. This vast sea of phallic symbols is believed to represent a religious fertility cult. Whole cities were bragging about how large their hands were.

At the largest temples, the coliseums, the most commonly found ruins in their country, thousands of devout followers would pay homage to Freud by eating a red, phallus shaped piece of meat, six inches long, clamped between two einkorn covers, no doubt a bizarre ritual that only a devote of Sigmund Freud would understand.

"Sometimes a cigar is just a cigar"
Freud

Following the cries of spiritual passion, worshipers across the entire nation partake of a sacred drink to kill the pain of living, or losing... or for no reason at all.

Of course, these temples require great manpower and expense, not to mention thousands of devoted worshipers to build these great temples, so all the worshipers eagerly give at the gate to participate in this homage; to demonstrate their faith and to seek the favor of the gods.

Some say mysterious "Sky Gods", known as Ancient Aliens, created all of this and then left, leaving no trace of their presence except for vague references from their follower's video depositories on the History Channel.

How could future archeologists possibly interpret this as anything other than football being our temples and stadiums and phallic symbols being our religion? Perhaps, they would be right.

More than this, the archeologists would have found many lessor gods celebrated throughout this primitive polytheistic culture. The names of their gods were celebrated in large letters that ordained the façade of their temples, which grew up as the center of every large street intersection; the gods of Wal-Mart, Kroger, Aldi, Target, Cosco, and more. A new upstart god, Amazon.com, seems to have been present only over the electric wires.

Wars appear to have been fought between the gods Wal-Mart and Amazon. The supernatural nature of these wars is clear from the fact that Amazon does not even appear to be real, but is only found over electrical wires coming from a magical place they called the "internet".

Each of these gods seem to have a retinue of familiar followers who returned to worship many times a week. As a token of respect for the gods the worshipers would leave bits of green paper or plastic cards symbolizing their allegiance to the gods, in homage to their gods, and take away the blessings of their gods. Priests at the door who welcome the worshipers would bless the patrons as they left, making sure they had all the blessings they needed.

Clearly, this primitive culture worshiped many gods. Polytheism, the worship of many gods, seem to be evident even in religions that claimed to be monotheists. One of those, Christianity, worships three gods; the Father, the Son, and the Holy Ghost (Mathew 28:19, John 5:7 KJV). Many claim these gods are all the same, a Holy Trinity, yet most pray to only one, the Son, and tend to ignore the Father. All of their story's center around the Son, not the Father. They seem to have a bias against the elderly.

One of their religions claims to believe in *"love thy neighbor"*, *"bless him who curses you"*, *"return good for evil"*, *"if a man smites you on one cheek, turn the other cheek"*. This is a remarkable insight for such a primitive people, as it shows a recognition of how fallible we all are. Yet the evidence is clear that these same people engage in anger, hate, and attacks on anyone who is different. This is evident from their politics, where the underlying hate of those who are different, including immigrants and people who are awake (woke?), is evident.

Half of their population seem to hate immigrants, even though the same people all came to this country as immigrants themselves. There appear to be only a few good Samaritans in this culture who would welcome immigrants from a different culture. Thank God we do not live in such a culture today.

There is no evidence of cannibalism in this culture. Although, in some of their religious ceremony this was evident in the past, as they symbolically eat the body of the Son, and follow that with a drink of sacred purple grapes.

Perhaps future psychologists will be able to decipher the extreme differences between their religions. There are an estimated 250 versions of Christianity, from the Holy Rollers to the Snake Handlers; not even counting the Jonestown 900 or the 39 members of the Heavens Gate, who committed suicide so they could be taken aboard a spaceship, piloted by Jesus Christ, hidden in the wake of the Hale-Bopp comet. Yes, really.

Each of these 250 versions believe that they have the one true version of Christianity, and the other 249 are mistaken, or misled, or downright evil, apparently condemned already for not following the correct version of their religion. Since each believes in the absolute certainty of the version they were taught as children, it becomes impossible for them to consider any other version; much like trying to read Chinese after learning English.

PART VI

WORLD'S OLDEST RELIGION MAY STILL EXIST: EVIDENCE FOR A RELIGIOUS CENTER

Back to "reality". Primitive religions today are based on a reverence for their own personal ancestors, often called "Ancestor Worship". As time went by, the trade center at Gobekli could have morphed into a more common religion, just as fads sweep through our world today. What may have begun as wooden structures, could have been replaced by stone pillars, as we know happened at Stonehenge.

There is evidence that suggests a religious meaning for the art. Pillars such as the vulture pillar, with a headless man carved at the base of the pillar, and no "heads"on the T shaped pillars may suggest a bizarre death ritual which is found in the same regions today. A similar painting is found on the wall at Çatalhöyük, where a headless man is surrounded by vultures.

https://www.naturepl.com/stock-photo-wall-art-from-anexcavated-room-known-as-the- vulture-shrine--with-theimage01460837.html

 To this day there are similar practices in this region known as "sky burials". Here, the dead are intentionally put out into the field to be picked clean of flesh by vultures before they are buried and the head may be removed for ceremonial purposes. If you want to see a modern example where this is still practiced go to Youtube.com and search for "Sky Burials". Find the one from Wilderness Films. https://www.youtube.com/watch?v=5H2NTEVsIsw

The previous video is living evidence that we may not be far from deciphering our past.

(This footage is part of the broadcast stock footage archive of Wilderness Films India Ltd.)

This video shows modern people feeding an actual flock, a very large flock, of apparently tame vultures, by encouraging them to feast on the bodies of their human dead. Before their dead relatives are given to the vultures, the flesh on their bodies are cut into pieces because the vultures cannot easily do this themselves.

After the bodies are stripped of flesh and cleaned, they can be put into burials or their heads might be removed and kept in the houses as a tribute to the deceased or for their presumed magic to assist the living. We see such removed heads, covered with plaster, with eyes of cowrie shells or white stones, at Jericho and Çatalhöyük. Like the bones of Christian saints that are preserved in our cathedrals, the bones of their ancestors were likely to be associated with power and the ability to help the living or cure disease.

Often called "ancestor worship", this probably had a more personal meaning and value to the people than what we think of as "worship". It seems to represent a belief that the parents, that they knew so well, were still present (at least in their mind) and that their ancestor's spirits could still help in their very difficult lives.

Living with the dead buried under our home may seem bizarre to Americans. Yet even today we find groups who engage in similar practices as far away as Indonesia. You will find practices that may be similar to Çatalhöyük in this video:

https://www.youtube.com/watch?v=X46F0Q0X3Eo

PART VII

CENTRAL PILLARS AND THE "BURIAL" OF GOBEKLI

When Klaus Schmidt did his early excavations, he found that the central pillars were still upright, even though the slot at the base where the bottom rested was only about 4 inches deep and sitting on bedrock. It is believed that Gobekli was intentionally buried, because only the dirt around the pillars kept some of them upright.

Even today, they must have timber and ropes in place to hold up the central pillars or they would fall and break. These timbers are ugly and restrict movement within the center. Is it likely that this was true originally?

It seems more likely that the central pillars originally supported a wooden roof, and the wooden roof supported the central pillars.

The important function of the T shape at the top of the T pillars would have simply been to allow ropes to secure the logs to the top of the T. The discovery of T-shaped pillars at many sites from Hazman Tepe to Navali Cori may only indicate that these buildings had a roof, not that they had religious significance.

The distance between each of the T pillars in the outer circle may represent the space that logs would have to be placed, to span the distance from one pillar to the next. Logs could then be placed in a circle, from pillar to pillar, around the outside pillars.

The most likely reason why there are two taller central pillars is that it would have allowed them to make a larger space, up to 20 meters across. Wooden poles would have been too short to reach all the way across by themselves, so they only had to reach from the outer ring to the central pillars. Timber could be run from one central pillar to the second. This allowed a larger room.

Additional timber would go from the outer circle of logs to the central pillars. If the space between the two central pillars were great enough, an oculus might have been left in the center for more light, like the hole in the roof of a Superdome.

The two-foot distance between the rock wall and the top of the T-shaped pillars in the circle could have served the function of raising the roof just enough for ventilation, 360 degrees, around the entire structure. It would have been a circular roof, with beams and branches woven together.

If the climate was much wetter back then, as is generally assumed, they would have needed a roof to keep the sunken structures from becoming the world's first prehistoric swimming pools/communal baths.

So why did they "bury" Gobekli? Possibly years later the sites were buried; after so many other sites grew up, like the corner grocery stores/trading centers, that they no longer needed to come all the way to Gobekli. In time, the roof rotted and the pillars began to lean.

We cannot know this for certain of course, but people still around the site may have "buried" the pillars just to keep them from collapsing; just as today we have put timber around the pillars to keep them upright.

In the "fill" used to bury the site, vast amounts of bones of aurochs, gazelle, and other "wild" animals were found. Many assume these were wild animals killed for a feast. Just as likely, these were bones from animals shepherds herded at Gobekli.

In one last, far-out suggestion, if you note the top of the "vulture" pillar you see three remarkable handbags; a precursor to Gucci? They look just like the ones found in carvings in much later reliefs throughout Mesopotamia, thousands of years later, and just like the reusable woven cloth shopping bags we see at Walmart. Did the people of Gobekli make woven shopping bags so others could carry their goods home? Or did they carry offerings and tribute? Or, are they the first "man-bag" for when we had no pockets? Or were they pails like the water pails common in America 100 years ago?

Ooops. I just saw an Olmec carving from La Venta, Tabasco, Mexico with a man carrying a nearly identical bag. Apparently, these are not all original Gucci's. Did Walmart model their reusable woven shopping bags from Gobekli? Or La Venta? Not likely. It seems this is such a natural design for a woven bag or water pail that everybody was making them the same way.

The previous picture is from Knossos in Crete 3,200 years ago. Note the two central pillars that seem nearly identical to the central pillars at Gobekli. Did they copy this from Gobekli? Or is this such a common way to support a roof, with ropes tied to the "T" to hold the roof in place, that, like the handbags or pails at Gobekli, it was in common use?

Most farmers would appreciate how difficult it is to keep their herds together, even with barbed wire. Could wooden corrals, that later became stone corrals, have been the major purpose for these sites? Possibly even the row after row of stone megaliths in France and elsewhere, may have first been marked off as corrals and spaces in their trading center. Centuries later, all the way through the mid1900s, the French would build extensive "hedgerows" of earth and stone as borders marking off their crops and livestock. They used earth, stone, and hedges to divide their property and keep their herds intact.

The evidence of groups of animals being kept at Stonehenge is not as good as the multiple, waist-high, doorless, rooms inside Gobekli's circles. If Stonehenge had corrals made of wood or a roof tied to the lintel stones on top of the sarsen stones, the wood has long since rotted away, leaving only our imagination.

The people who were good at working stone, might have been spectacular at working wood. But the wood has disappeared, leaving us to only guess at what we have missed.

In the 1980s 40 circular impressions, about 40' wide were discovered in Austria. They dated to 6,000 years old. Wolfgang Neubauer an archeologist at Ludwig Boltzmann Institute, (Neubauer discovered that Stonehenge had originally been built of wood.), went on to reconstructed one of the other European circular enclosures, using close-fitting timbers.

It ended up looking very much like a double ring of circular pens which could have held cattle or sheep, with the narrow width between the walls being useful in keeping the sheep or cattle calm, reduce fighting, and channel them in one direction toward the Pez style exit. However, there is no apparent agreement as to the function of these circular pens.

WHY THE DOUBLE WALLS IN WOODEN STRUCTURES IN EUROPE?

Many believe that the double wall may have been used for defense, which is perfectly logical. Yet the double wall recreated by Neubauer looks like it would have been impossible to use a spear or bow and arrow over the tall pillars.

It could have been for defense, yet a double ring of posts close to the outer ring, is remarkably similar to Gobekli's structure C and the circular chutes of Dr. Grandin. Some of the megalithic stones that still stand at hundreds of sites in Europe may have had wood or rock structures in between them making them useful as corrals or holding pens, or just to mark off the spots that those who came to barter would use.

The wood would rot, and the smaller rocks might have been removed for use in building elsewhere, leaving us with no clear picture of what they might originally have been used for; as happened when the Spanish reused the stones in Cuzco and other Inca cities to build their churches and courts.

PART VIII

WHOEVER CONTROLLED THE TRADE, CONTROLLED THE FUTURE

In summary, the great mistake of archeologists in interpreting Gobekli as built by Hunter-Gatherers, seems to have come from the belief that the Aurochs, Gazelles, sheep, and pig bones found at Gobekli, came from Hunter-Gatherers, because they found no bones from "domesticated" animals.

- Instead, it seems more likely that they used "Imprinting" to attach the young animals they found to themselves.

- By catching very young animals, breeding them in corrals, and eating the older ones, they eventually, by accident, turned the animals into "domesticated" looking animals by a process of artificially selecting the more docile animal to keep and breed, and the more "wild" and rambunctious animals were eaten first.

- Animal Husbandry is likely to have provided the basis of the food supply essential to the large settlements around Gobekli and the building of Gobekli itself.

- Much of what we call the late Hunter-Gather period throughout the world may have brought people together by offering, at first, a central place to trade their goods. Petra, Gobekli, Stonehenge, seem likely to have begun as large "wet" markets, or flea markets where people from miles away came to barter anything they could catch, grow, breed or make.

- The purpose of the stone structures likely varied. Smaller stone structures may have been individual houses. Other stone structures may have been corrals to contain the animals, making them readily available without the risk of failures from hunting.

- Larger stone structures, especially those at Gobekli, are likely to have offered, not just trade, but socializing, mating opportunities, exchanging ideas, fads, the spread of new grains and more. Shamans likely provided story telling and religious beliefs, the movies of their day.

- Even the great empires of the Egyptians, Aztecs, Inca and Maya may have begun in their own wet markets. Whoever controlled the trade, controlled the future. They may have become rulers; the top 1%.

- Their shopping mall security force, the bouncers, may have become their army. As thousands of years went by, they may have morphed into religious centers, city-states and eventually, empires.

VIII: EPILOGUE

It is no longer enough to be an expert in one field. Psychologists who know nothing about the great work of cultural anthropologists like Ruth Benedict, Margaret Mead, Clyde Kluckhohn, understand nothing about the enormous variety of human behavior. Psychologists who do not understand archeology, cannot easily imagine the environment that made us who we are.

By the same token, archeologists who miss the value of psychology may also miss what is hidden in plain sight; the ease with which "wild" animals can be tamed if you start with imprinting their babies first, which would have been essential *before* they could select for "domesticated" animals. The psychological reasons for needing a narrow, circular, double-walled pen is evident. That keeps the cattle or sheep, or maybe pigs and gazelles, moving in one direction, reduces fighting, and keeps them calm. It helps to have more than one discipline involved in interpreting reality.

Or, maybe, just ask a cowboy.

David Lloyd Shepard

David Lloyd Shepard is a textbook author with 15 years' experience as an associate clinical psychologist and 21 years teaching psychology. He has written four books including *FORCES OF LIFE: Psychology and Success or Failure in Ourselves and our Children, MIND: Psychology—The Untold Story*, and *PSYCHOLOGY: The Science of Human Behavior.* Now, *The New PSYCHOLOGY; A Unified Field of Brain, Mind, Behavior, Culture, Perception, and Life...*

ACKNOWLEDGMENTS

Photos licensed from Depositphotos

Gobekli illustration by bhupeshpaikra

Drawing licensed from Squidphotos

Photos courtesy Dr. Temple Grandin

Profound appreciation for all who have come before.

Apologies if I have missed anyone.

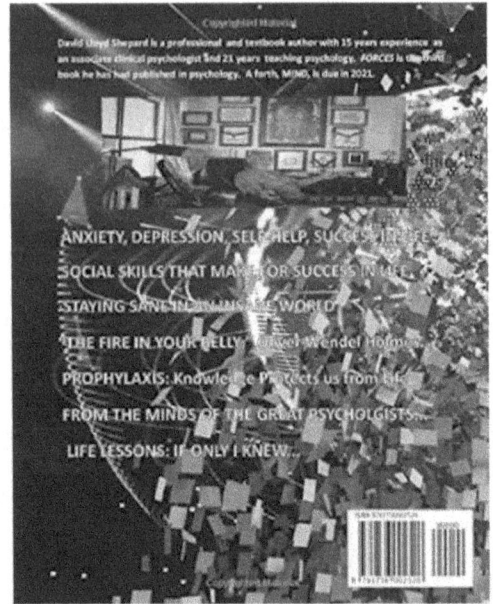

351 pages. Psychology, Counseling, and Education are at a "tipping point" on the edge of an active volcano. In the 1970s an average of 25,000 Americans a year committed suicide. Today, that figure stands at 48,000 per year, every year, _before_ the job loss from Covid-19 began in 2020.

Even though we now have six times more psychologists, psychiatrists, and school councilors than we had then, and about as great an increase in anti-depressive medication, we have failed massively. Unhappiness in life is epidemic. Our schools now have police watching our children. Where did we go wrong?

"The only defense against the world is a thorough knowledge of it." John Locke.

We could easily use the existing educational system for a program of preventive psychology based on the better principles of psychology by the best minds in psychology. Albert Bandura, in an almost unknown experiment, found he could use modeling *films* to prevent panic and counter the fear of dogs in forty children, simply by showing them *films* of a happy boy and a dog. We can use some of the methods in this book to accomplish a similar success with 40 or 400 children or adults at once, something no individual counseling can accomplish.

By combining two of the best scientific methods, Systematic Observation, as used by Copernicus, Galileo, Einstein, Alexander Fleming, Jane Goodall and Margaret Mead, with the Experiments of Albert Bandura and others, it is possible to transform the problems of life for the better. We can deal with cyberbullying, feelings of failure, anxiety, depression, prejudice and more.

Anxiety, Depression, Self-Help, Social Skills, Success: What is it the greatest minds in psychology and those who are the most successful in life know about success and failure? How can we use this knowledge to prevent problems and increase success? Knowledge is a key to success and to surviving failure.

"If only I knew then, what I know now…" is the most common regret of life. It fairly screams the critical importance of knowledge, yet there are few sources to learn from.

Knowledge and understanding can change your brain as effectively as any therapy. Preventing psychological problems can be more effective than treating them after they occur. This book is about how learning from others can protect ourselves and our children from the pain of living and learn the social skills and knowledge that make us successful in our personal lives, raising our children, our families.

This book is an attempt to provide the understanding we need for ourselves and our children to do well in a world that often makes no sense, is often irrational, and difficult to understand. In their own words, we will read about the experiences that inspired the lives and success of others that help give us a hint at a blueprint of life.

See at: https://www.amazon.com/dp/173600252X

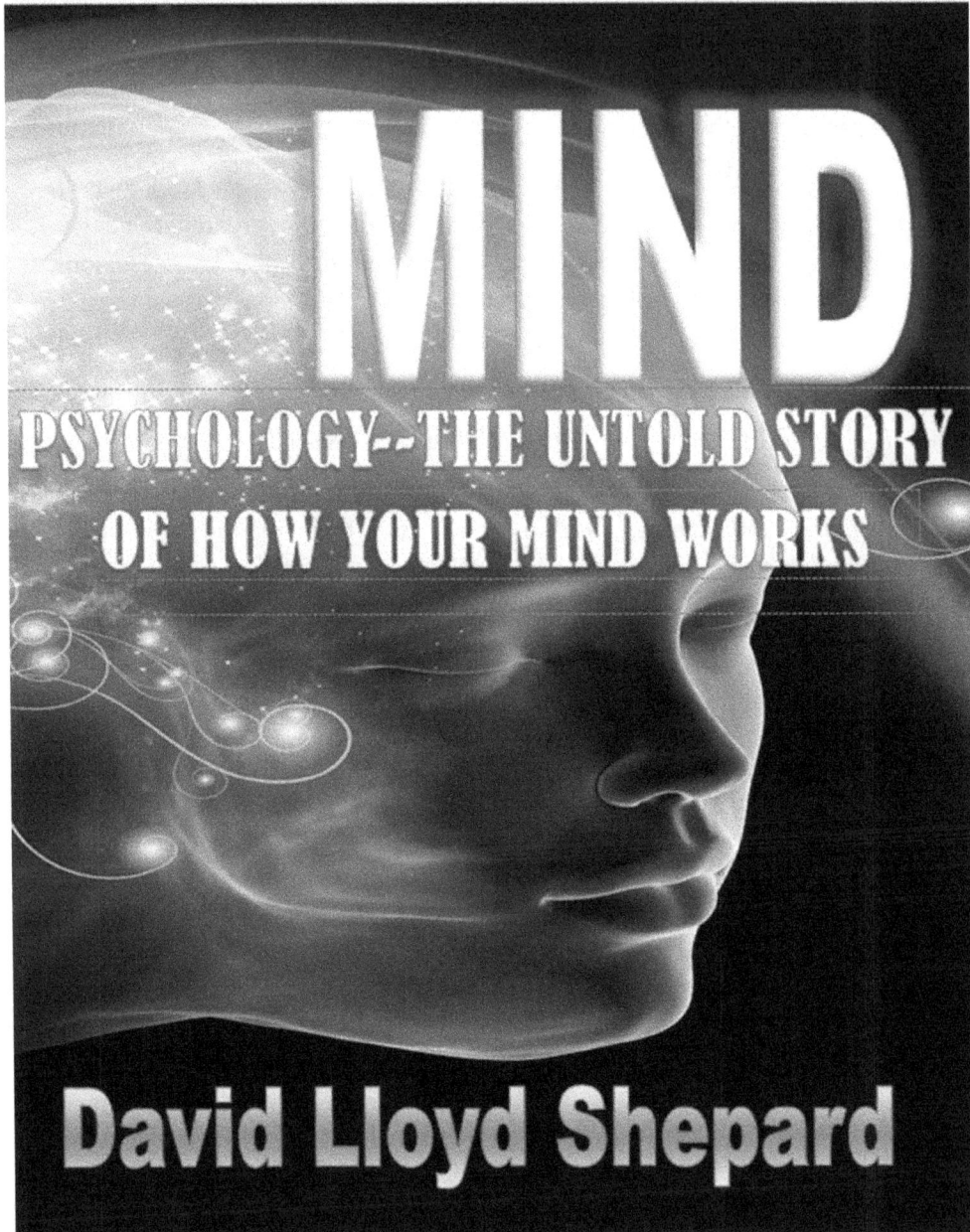

MIND

PSYCHOLOGY--THE UNTOLD STORY OF HOW YOUR MIND WORKS

David Lloyd Shepard

360 pages. This is a book about the most important discoveries in psychology. Not just the stories in a textbook, but what has been left out of our textbooks.

How is it that the greatest minds in history were able to make some of the most astonishing discoveries of all time when others could not? How is it that others reacted with anger to the greatest discoveries of all time?

All of us want to read about the amazing, secret, hidden powers of the mind. This book is often about the opposite; not just the genius of the mind but the other 99.99% of reality, the part left out of our education

MIND: Psychology—The Untold Story of How Your Mind Works

GENIUS IS IN THE MIND, NOT THE BRAIN. The Success of Genius is in Learning How to Think, not in your biology. How the greatest minds in history made their discoveries in their own words.

TEST YOUSELF: Do you think like a Genius?

COGITO, ERGO, COGITO, COGITO: I Think, Therefore, I Think I Think. The fact that we can think has created the illusion that we do think.

QUEST FOR THE MIND CODE: Psychology's General Theory of Relativity.

BEYOND THE SINGULARITY: When our Laws no Longer Apply

MIND CONTROL: An Everyday Occurrence, Kamakazie pilots, Suicide Bombers, Politics, Celebrity, etc.

THE BRAIN: How Experience Hardwires the Brain

UNDERSTANDING HOW THE MIND WORKS GIVE US THE POTENTIAL TO CONTROL OUR OWN MIND.

AVAILABLE NOW: https://www.amazon.com/dp/1736002554

www.ingramcontent.com/pod-product-compliance
Lightning Source LLC
Chambersburg PA
CBHW081724270326
41933CB00017B/3283